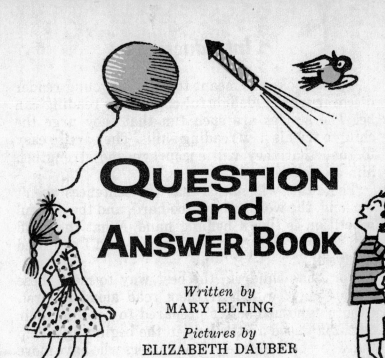

QUESTION and ANSWER BOOK

Written by
MARY ELTING

Pictures by
ELIZABETH DAUBER

Editorial Consultant:
LILIAN MOORE

Technical Adviser:
THEODORE MARTON, Ph.D.

Wonder® Books
PRICE/STERN/SLOAN
Publishers, Inc., Los Angeles
1984

Introduction

These books are meant to help the young reader discover what a delightful experience reading can be. The stories are such fun that they urge the child to try his new reading skills. They are so easy to read that they will encourage and strengthen him as a reader.

The adult will notice that the sentences aren't too long, the words aren't too hard, and the skillful repetition is like a helping hand. What the child will feel is: "This is a good story—and I can read it myself!"

For some children, the best way to meet these stories may be to hear them read aloud at first. Others, who are better prepared to read on their own, may need a little help in the beginning—help that is best given freely. Youngsters who have more experience in reading alone—whether in first or second or third grade—will have the immediate joy of reading "all by myself."

These books have been planned to help all young readers grow—in their pleasure in books and in their power to read them.

Lilian Moore
Specialist in Reading
Formerly of Division of Instructional Research,
New York City Board of Education

Illustrations Copyright © 1963, 1981 by Price/Stern/Sloan Publishers, Inc.
Text Copyright © 1953 by Mary Elting
Published by Price/Stern/Sloan Publishers, Inc.
410 North La Cienega Boulevard, Los Angeles, California 90048

ISBN: 0-8431-4317-7
Wonder® Books is a trademark of Price/Stern/Sloan Publishers, Inc.

What Is Lightning?

Lightning is electricity.

Lightning is a very big spark
of electricity.

You can make some lightning.

How?

Do this:

Brush your hair
in a dark room.
Brush very hard.
You will see little sparks.
They are little sparks
of electricity.

Lightning is a
very, very big spark
of electricity.

Snap! Snap! Snap!

When you brush,

you make little snaps.

They are little bits of thunder.

9

What Is Thunder?

Lightning makes thunder.

Lightning makes the air very hot.

When air gets hot, it spreads out.

It expands.

It expands very fast.

The hot air bumps into cool air.

It bumps hard.

PUSH! PUSH! PUSH!

Hot air is pushing on cool air.

Air that pushes hard makes noise.

Thunder is nothing but

a very big noise.

Why Do Rabbits Have Big Ears?

A rabbit has big ears

and long, strong legs.

His big ears listen.

His long legs go fast.

His big ears turn this way

and that way—

up and down.

They hear everything.

Listen!

What is that?

Is that a fox?

Or a man?

Or only
a mouse?

A rabbit's big ears tell him "RUN!"

Why Do Teeth Come Out?

When you were a baby,

you had little teeth.

Your teeth were just the right size

for a baby.

You grew bigger,

but your teeth did not grow.

Baby teeth stay the same size.

New teeth grow under baby teeth.

The new teeth grow and push.

At last they push the baby teeth

out of the way.

Big new teeth come in.

Your new teeth

are just the right size for you.

Baby animals get new teeth, too.

What Is an Orbit?

Away goes a space man.
Soon he is high
over the earth.

Around the earth he goes—
around and around and around,
in a big loop.
This big loop is like a path
around the earth.

The space man's path
around the earth
is called an orbit.
The moon goes around the earth
in an orbit, too.
And the earth moves in an orbit
around the sun.

What Is a Satellite?

A satellite goes around and around
in space.

It goes around in an orbit.

A satellite always goes
around something bigger.

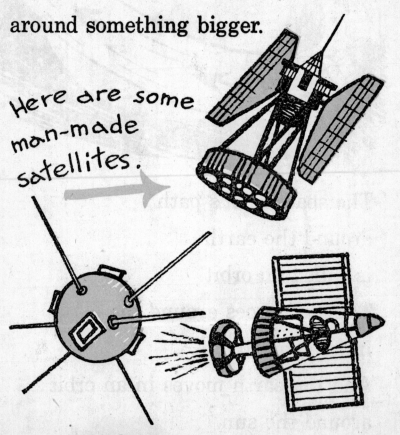

Here are some
man-made
satellites.

18

What Can a Satellite Do?

This little satellite goes
around and around the earth.
It is a weather satellite.
Men made it
and sent it up into space.
A weather satellite
can take TV pictures
of the clouds.

What for?

TV pictures of the clouds tell us
what the weather will be!

The moon is a satellite.

It goes around

and around the earth.

The earth goes around

and around, too.

The earth goes around the sun.

Is the earth a satellite?

Yes.

You are riding on a satellite

right now!

21

Do Animals Talk to One Another?

The mother cat goes "Meow!"

Her baby hears and comes running.

"Meow!"

One dog goes "Grrrrr!"

The other dog runs away.

"Grrrrr!"

The mother duck goes "Quack!"

The baby ducks follow her.

"Quack"

Animals make noises,
but they do not really talk.
They cannot say,
"Two and two are four."
They cannot tell jokes.
Only people can really talk
to one another.

What <u>bus</u> crossed the ocean?

COLUMB<u>US</u>!

What Are Germs?

Germs are very, very tiny.

They are so tiny that

you cannot see them.

But the doctor can see them.

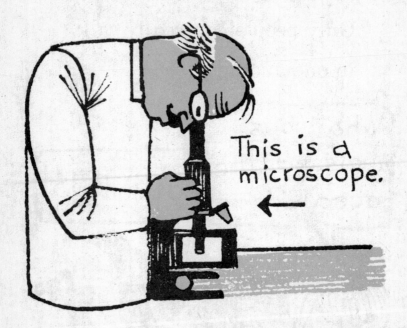

This is a microscope.

He sees them with a microscope.

A microscope makes tiny things

look big.

The doctor can see germs
with his microscope.
Germs are living things.

They can grow.

Some germs make us sick.

We put medicine on a cut

so that germs cannot get

under the skin and make us sick.

Does Anyone Live on the Moon?

Nobody lives on the moon.

The moon has no air.

Rain never falls on the moon.

No plants grow on the moon.

There is nothing to eat.

So nobody lives on the moon now.

What Happens to Stars in the Daytime?

Do stars go away in the daytime?

No.

They are still in the sky.

They are still sending out light.

But in the daytime,

the sun sends out light, too.

The sun makes the air shine.

That is why the sky

is so bright in the daytime

that we cannot see the stars.

How Does Soap Make Your Hands Clean?

Soap and water

make hands clean.

Soap helps water.

It helps to make dirt soft.

When dirt is soft,

it cannot stick to your hands.

Soap bubbles help to pick up

tiny bits of dirt

and make them float away.

How Does a Submarine Go Down?

A submarine has big tanks inside.

When the tanks are full of air,

the submarine stays up.

Sometimes the men in a submarine

want to go down.

Then they let water into the tanks.

The water pushes the air out.

The submarine goes down,

down.

Sea water

Sea water

Sea water

How Does a Submarine Come Up?

When air is blown into the tanks,

it pushes the water out.

The submarine comes up.

TRY THIS:

Fill a paper cup with water.

It will go down.

Now turn the cup over

and blow like this:

See what happens!

What Happened to the Dinosaurs?

Once there were many dinosaurs.

They were all over the earth.

How do we know?

We still find old dinosaur bones

and old dinosaur eggs.

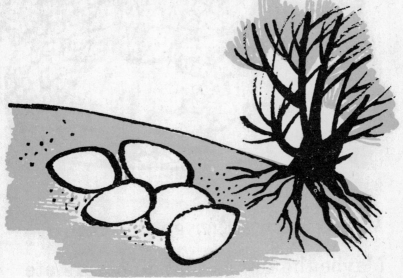

But there are no dinosaurs

on the earth now.

What happened?

Maybe the weather got too cool.

Maybe the things that dinosaurs ate

could not grow.

Then they had no more food.

Or maybe this happened—

Some new animals came
and lived where dinosaurs lived.
Some of these new animals
liked to eat dinosaur eggs.

Maybe THAT was the end
of the dinosaurs!

How Does a Rocket Work?

You can make yourself go

like a rocket.

You need skates and a big ball.

Put on the skates.

Now hold the ball in both hands

and push it.

When you push a ball,

the ball seems to give you a push.

It seems to push you back.

Push the ball again.

Again, the ball goes one way,

and you go the other way.

A rocket does this, too. How?

A hot fire makes a rocket go.

The fire makes lots of hot gas.

This hot gas pushes out
of the rocket.

The hot gas goes one way,
and the rocket
goes the other way.

The inside
of a rocket
looks something
like this.

The hot gas goes very fast.

So does the rocket.

Down goes the hot gas.

Up goes the rocket—very fast!

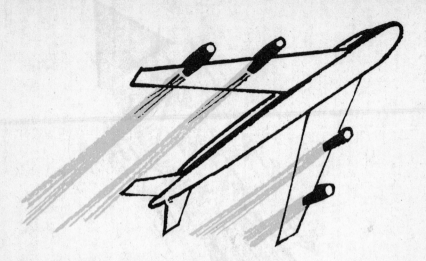

Is a Jet Like a Rocket?

A jet works something like a rocket.

A rocket needs a hot fire inside.

So does a jet.

Hot gas pushes out of a rocket

and out of a jet, too.

A rocket goes very fast.

So does a jet.

But a jet and a rocket

are not the same.

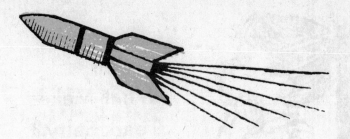

A jet can only fly

where there is air.

A rocket can fly anywhere.

It can fly out in space,

where there is no air at all!

What Makes
Tears Salty?

There is real salt in tears.

It is like the salt

that you put into food.

There is salt in your body.

The salt and water in your body

make tears.

Why Does a Cat Wash?

Nobody tells a cat to wash.

A cat does not have to think
about washing.

A cat just does it.

Many animals wash.

Maybe clean faces feel better.

wire worm

45

Where Do Insects Go in Winter?

 These insects fly away
to warm places
in winter.

Ants stay in a nest
under the earth.

 Some bees live in a house
that the farmer makes
for them.

This insect swims around in water
under the ice.

This one makes a leaf
into a sleeping bag.

Then it sleeps
inside the bag
all winter long.

These babies sleep all winter
in a piece of wood.

Some insects die
when winter comes.

chirp
chirp

This insect makes a little cave
or hides in somebody's house.

We do not know
where some insects go.
Maybe they hide
and we cannot see them.

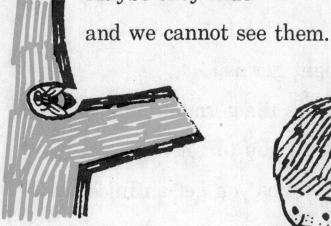

Look for them.
Maybe you can find out
where they go.

Why Does the Doctor
Give Injections?

Some germs make you sick.

Your body can fight these germs.

But sometimes

your body needs help.

An injection helps your body

to fight germs.

It keeps the germs from growing.

It helps you to get well.

Sometimes you get an injection

when you are NOT sick.

This injection is a

germ fighter, too.

It helps you to stay well.

It helps your body to stop germs
before they can make you sick.
It is a stay-well injection.

What Are Tails For?

A tail can help.

A tail can help a cow.

A tail can help a monkey.

A tail can do this:

or this:

swish

But some tails

do not seem to do anything at all!

Why Are Some Leaves Yellow in Fall?

Leaves are green in summer.

The green color grows

inside the leaves.

There is yellow color

inside the leaves, too.

But the green hides the yellow.

In fall the tree stops making

green color.

Then we can see the yellow.

How Is Spaghetti Made?

First, people do this:

Then they do this:

Mix! Mix! Mix!
They are mixing flour
into a dough.
They will make
the dough
into
spaghetti.

Now they put the dough
into a big tank.
The tank has little holes in it.

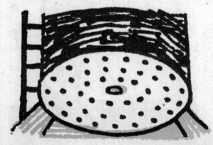

What are
the holes for?

Push! Push! Push!
The dough is pushed
out of the holes.

Next, a big knife
cuts the spaghetti.

Then the spaghetti is hung up to dry.

Round holes make round spaghetti.

And these holes make ABC's for soup!

How Do People Find Answers?

People like to find answers.

They like to look

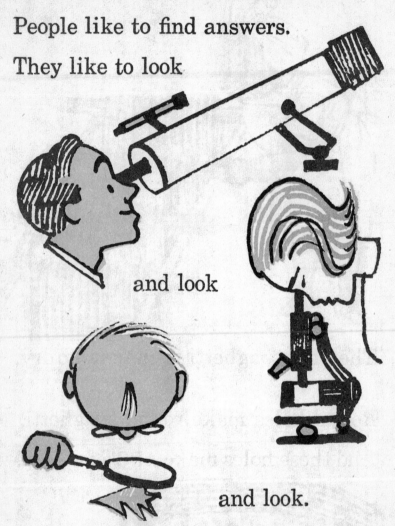

and look

and look.

They try things.

They think.

You can look.

You can try.

You can think.

You can find answers, too.